THE COUNTRY CUPBOARD

FLOWERS

THE COUNTRY CUPBOARD

FLOWERS

IMAGINATIVE TIPS & SENSIBLE ADVICE

FOR SELECTING, ARRANGING, & ENJOYING

PAT ROSS

Watercolors by Carolyn Bucha

FRIEDMAN/FAIRFAX
PUBLISHERS

A FRIEDMAN/FAIRFAX BOOK

Library of Congress Cataloging-in-Publication data available upon request.

ISBN 1-56799-729-5

Editor: Reka Simonsen
Art Director: Jeff Batzli
Designer: Andrea Karman
Production Director: Karen Matsu Greenberg

Printed in Hong Kong by Midas Printing Ltd.

1 3 5 7 9 10 8 6 4 2

For bulk purchases and special sales, please contact:
Friedman/Fairfax Publishers
Attention: Sales Department
15 West 26th Street
New York, New York 10010
212/685-6610
FAX 212/685-1307

Visit our website:
http://www.metrobooks.com

Acknowledgments

There's flower power behind *Flowers*. Bouquets of thanks go to my many talented friends who took time to answer the seemingly endless little questions that arose when I figured out the true meaning of "knowing just enough to be dangerous" while writing about flower arranging.

Evan G. Hughes is a cutting-edge floral designer from Connecticut who—with his spontaneously natural arrangements—showed the rest of us how to break away from stuffy displays. He's also a friend who went through the manuscript twice with a fine-tooth comb, no doubt getting some of the smart comments from Peter Ermacora.

How fortunate I am to have more than one or two creative friends who work with flowers daily. Arkansas artist and designer Charles Muise—with the support of Gene Heil—offered countless imaginative ideas on the creation of containers and arrangements that enliven the pages of this book.

My publisher, Michael Friedman, my tireless editor Sharyn Rosart, and the staff at Michael Friedman Publishing Group have such savvy and energetic ideas. My quick copyeditor Barbara Clark always makes good sense of my thoughts. I've been privileged to have Carolyn Bucha's delightful drawings in three of my books so far—a sure sign of kinship, floral and otherwise.

Long-stemmed roses to Margie Haber and Charlotte Frishkorn, my gardening friends who answered questions and gave support. Ellen Platt, a friend as well as an expert on dried flowers, was always available to share her wisdom. Then there's Ken McGraw, who never fails to remember just how much I love flowers.

Contents

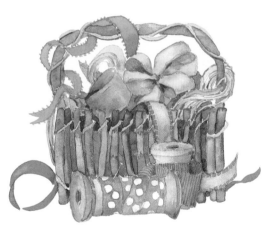

Introduction

A room with flowers is a lived-in place. Not a week passes that I don't arrange fresh flowers for a certain table that would look undressed without them. When I go grocery shopping, I look for the biggest bunches of parsley and sage so that I'll have sprigs left over to pop into a pretty glass or two on the sleek marble counter. My neighborhood in New York is filled with flower shops and greengrocers whose beautiful wares—pushed as far into the walkways as the law allows—can brighten even the dreariest city days and never fail to lift my spirits. When the weather turns warm and breezy, I head downtown to an open-air market where the myriad containers of exuberant flowers have the power to drag people right off passing buses.

The cutting garden at our farm in Virginia is still a bare work-in-progress, though I rarely go wanting for flowers there. Jonquils and daisies were planted years ago by former owners whose nonchalant style of gardening has resulted in curious clumps of seasonal color around the house. Romantic peonies and brilliant purple irises grow in an abandoned farmhouse garden next door, and black-eyed Susans bloom everywhere. Our fields and woodland are filled with Queen Anne's lace, colorful wildflowers I am learning to name, and all the twigs, berries, and branches that I could possibly desire. Even in the deep freeze of Shenandoah Mountain winters, I find evergreens to fill the house with their heady fragrance.

I rarely go to a crafts show without buying a new vase. I am always amazed by the mind-boggling array of containers, old and new. A vibrant blue glaze can set off sunflowers;

a much-loved terra-cotta pitcher speaks of earth and the elements; an elegant Lalique vase says "lights, action, drama." Peach-colored roses paired with a crystal vase always make a winning combination, yet I find that the same roses in a weathered pail can be dazzling. So over the years, I've simply had a wonderful time with flowers.

When I began work on my first design book, *Formal Country*, I realized the photographs needed that extra touch that only flowers can provide. Suddenly, it was up to me to create picture-perfect arrangements, meant to be published! I had never thought much about what I knew—or didn't know—about flower arranging. I panicked, feeling entirely unqualified. Fortunately, my good friend Evan G. Hughes is a noted floral designer who conducts lectures on flower arranging.

Evan's arrangements are always magnificently loose and carefree, as though the flowers had just happily arranged themselves. The spontaneous and casual way he works with flowers is almost playful, poking a branch here and a bloom there, never stiff or too showy. Luckily, he came to the rescue with some sensible advice. "Think of it this way," he said. "If you learn a few basics about caring for fresh flowers, how can you fail with beautiful snapdragons or a perfect rose?"

I've found that flower arranging is a pleasure, as long as I keep it simple. If I have only a few minutes in an otherwise chaotic week, I opt for pretty tulips in a vase that's worked before, or I choose the most magnificent single flower I can find. When I'm feeling more adventuresome, I work with flowers that are new to me. I've found that flower arranging becomes a pleasurable part of every week if I remember that flowers are simply an extension of my decor, my lifestyle, and my personality.

I recently met an old friend at the airport who had just traveled from California with magnificent antique roses from her beloved garden as a gift just for me. Wrapped in soggy newspaper, most of the roses had survived heroically. The makeshift wrapping and a few droopy roses didn't for a moment diminish my friend's joyful gesture.

–Pat Ross

chapter one

Floral Basics

THE RIGHT STUFF:
A LIST OF ESSENTIAL TOOLS AND MATERIALS

You yearn for a simple vase of cheerful tulips in January or decide to arrange the flowers for your daughter's big wedding. In either case, there's no need to fill a spare room with a florist's tools of the trade. But it is good sense to have a variety of essential tools of professional quality to get started. Not even the most creative spirit gets very far when cutting flowers with a butter knife. The more you develop your skills with the right equipment and tools, the easier and more enjoyable flower arranging will be.

This list begins with the smart basics and moves on to things you may need when your skills and interests expand.

Scissors: A pair of sharp scissors will come in handy for soft stems, ribbon, tape, and the like. When you cut hard stems with scissors, you may squeeze stems instead of making a clean cut, and you risk losing valuable plant cells.

Pruning Shears: A pair of pruning shears is the best tool for cutting fresh flowers, especially those with woody stems. Keep them handy in a garden basket, and always keep them sharp.

Sharp Knife: A small, sharp knife such as a paring knife is useful for cutting hard woody stems and for removing bumps, thorns, and unwanted material from stems, as well as for shaping floral foam to fit a container.

Gloves: A pair of comfortable garden gloves is essential—flexible and well fitted, yet heavy-duty enough to protect against those thorny roses. A great part of the enjoyment is handling the flowers.

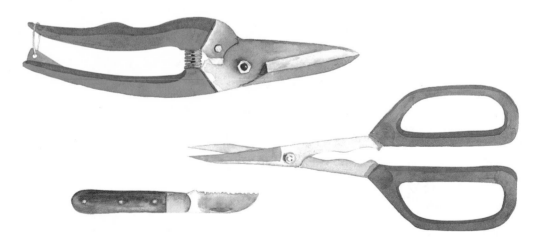

Floral Foam (also referred to as Oasis): Floral foam is soaked in water and used wet, and comes in dark green, gray, and brown. It is easily cut to fit a container or special arrangement.

Styrofoam: Available in blocks of every imaginable shape (stars, crosses, balls, circles, and more), Styrofoam creates a decorative base, especially for dry arrangements.

Florist Clay: Its uses include securing Styrofoam to a container or floral frogs in a vase. It also helps ensure that trays and saucers hold tightly to the bottoms of their containers, as when using a terracotta pot.

Florist Tape: A waterproof tape, usually dark green or brown, that is used to secure floral foam to containers and to create grids over container openings.

Clear Adhesive Tape: This tape is primarily used for making grids over the openings of containers when a less visible tape is needed. Look for a waterproof type.

> A bowl of roses in the living room...does far more than please the eye and regale the nose; it distinctly enlivens the atmosphere and revives the occupants of the room.
>
> Louise Beebe Wilder

Corsage Tape: Self-sticking paper tape, available in green and brown, is used to bind wires to stems as well as to wrap bundles of stems.

String or Light Cord: String is helpful for many tasks, including tying bunches.

Chicken Wire: Medium-gauge wire can be crumpled and inserted into a container, laid over the top, or wrapped over floral foam for extra support. Avoid wire with a gauge that is too small for stems to be inserted easily. You might also consider plastic-coated wire for the protection it offers more delicate flowers.

Plastic: A large piece of plastic sheeting will keep your work area clean and make it easy to tidy up. Small pieces of plastic are necessary for lining containers as protection against water seepage.

Plastic Bowls: It's never too soon to begin collecting a variety of plastic bowls—bought especially to fit inside a particular vase or left over from last night's takeout—to use as liners. Don't forget empty food containers, such as those from cottage cheese or sour cream, as well as waxy milk cartons in various sizes.

Floral Reel Wire: It's helpful to have very fine silver reel wire as well as a medium-gauge reel wire in green or black to secure, bind, or add flowers or foliage to an arrangement.

Floral Straight Wire: These straight lengths of wire, used primarily to reinforce stems, are available in a variety of thicknesses. Select a medium-gauge wire to begin with.

Bottle or Vase Brush: A brush is important for getting narrow containers clean of bacteria. Buy a big all-purpose brush as well as a smaller one for diminutive containers and narrow-necked vases.

Floral Frog: A frog is a holder, often made of glass or pottery, that contains many small holes to hold stems securely. It is placed in the bottom of a bowl or container.

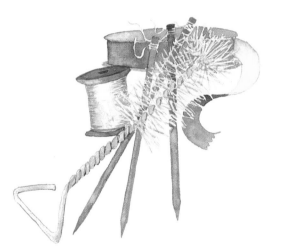

Wire- and Pincushion-Type Holders:
Generally made of heavy metal, wire- and
pincushion-type holders provide a stable
base for inserting and positioning stems.
The loop styles do not pierce the stems.
Collapsible wire designs can be stored
conveniently.

Garden Sticks: Available in a variety of
lengths and sizes, sticks provide support
for tall, fragile stems.

HOMEWARD BOUND: TRANSPORTING CUT FLOWERS SUCCESSFULLY

I've been known to belt up for the long
trip from Virginia to New York with a
mason jar of tulips in my lap, check in for
a flight with peonies as my main baggage, and become a hazard to pedestri-
ans with my arms full of long forsythia
branches. Even though I know my
favorite flower shop near my New York
City apartment will have fresh and rea-
sonably priced daisies by the hundreds, I
just can't resist picking the daisies that
beckon to me in my country garden.

There are certain instances when
having flowers arrive in good shape—for a
garden benefit, a club luncheon, or a church
service—is especially important. Tailor the
methods to suit the occasion.

Ten cloudy days may pass over a garden without winning a flower, but no sooner does the sun shine, than hundreds of roses open upon the air. Good cheer divides our burdens and carries many of them; so farewell to all discouragement.

from the Shaker publication *The Manifesto*

◆ Choose flowers at the bud stage rather than full blooms, as the buds have a better chance of surviving a trip. Full-blown flowers can look ravishing, but are chancy for the long haul.

◆ Be sure to cut and trim flowers properly. Flowers that have received some care and conditioning ahead of time are much better travelers.

◆ Recut and condition flowers as soon as you reach your destination.

◆ If there's room on the floor of the car, you can wrap individual stems in tissue paper or paper towels dampened with a spray-mister. A box to hold the flowers is helpful; make sure it's long enough to hold the flowers straight. On very hot or dry days, I sometimes tuck a small spray-mister in my tote bag to dampen the paper when it begins to get dry.

◆ A heavy plastic bag can hold a large quantity of water without springing leaks if the bag is closed around the bouquet tightly with string or a big rubber band. Use such a bag in combination with damp tissue or paper towels.

◆ My mason jar method also works with an old glass jug or a plastic container. Fill the container at least halfway. Prevent splashes by gently crushing tinfoil around the stems and over the sides of the container.

◆ Tall containers, like the ones in the florist's refrigerator that are designed to hold and condition flowers, can stand behind a car seat or in the back of a van. Wedge or brace them carefully to avoid tipping when the vehicle turns. Plastic milk crates work well to secure several of these florist's containers. You can also use empty plastic half-gallon milk containers with the tops cut off.

✦ Many airlines I've encountered are not thrilled with my newspaper-wrapped bundles. However, the attendants are far more hospitable if I've encased the damp, paper-wrapped bouquet in a plastic bag or tinfoil. Flowers may be your idea of carry-on baggage, but if the flight is crowded, be prepared to hold bouquets.

✦ A short trip with a gift of flowers is the easiest to accomplish. Keep a roll of clear cellophane on hand so that you can spiral it loosely around your bouquet and still see the flowers and greens. Tie the bouquet with a ribbon that picks up one of the colors in the arrangement. When you wrap it, allow the flower heads to breathe. A large gift arrangement should be covered completely to protect it, especially if some of the flowers are very fragile. Just be certain to poke breathing holes in the cellophane or tissue.

✦ Get to know the flowers that travel well and the varieties that simply do not. I've had great luck transporting peonies, daisies, and black-eyed Susans, but little with lilacs and roses. Irises also are a bit touchy.

FIRST THINGS FIRST: SELECTING, CUTTING, AND CONDITIONING

As a child, I can remember my mother letting me pop an aspirin into the water of her fading flower arrangement to perk it up—one of many floral old wives' tales. Since then, I've heard of countless little "remedies"—lemonade, bleach, and gin among them. What the effective ones have in common is the presence of a small amount of sugar for nourishment, or an ingredient that cuts down on bacteria caused by rotting leaves and stems.

The way you cut fresh flowers— or recut flowers bought from a flower shop or open-air market—will have a great bearing on their appearance and longevity. The cutting combined with the essential cleaning and feeding (referred to as the conditioning of flowers) can make all the difference between a brief bow and several curtain calls.

Selecting

✦ Look for buds that are just beginning to open so that you can enjoy your flowers for many days, perhaps even weeks. Green buds that are too tight will droop rather than open. Avoid cutting and purchasing fully open blooms unless an occasion or an arrangement requires instant mature blooms and fullness.

✦ Healthy, dark green stems and leaves are signs of flowers with lasting power. Beware of pale leaves, fading and pale petals, and weak stems.

✦ When buying from greengrocers and open markets, look for merchants who have a quick turnover. Beware of "specials" and "sales" of prepackaged bouquets. Check for a fresh appearance, especially during hot spells. Be sure to look carefully to avoid broken stems and heads. Frequently, outdoor vendors receive their fresh flowers on one or more set days of the week. Inquire so that you'll be there for the pick of the crop.

✦ Get to know the florist in your neighborhood, and don't be timid about asking questions regarding the condition and care of the flowers you buy. Ask when certain flowers were delivered or how long they've been in the refrigeration unit. You may be paying top dollar for a dozen rare parrot tulips or several stems of exquisite bird-of-paradise, so it's your prerogative to know. When flowers that have been refrigerated for a while hit the real world, they often fade or droop. The refrigeration provides flowers with a near state of suspended animation, but they are still slowly deteriorating.

✦ When buying certain flowers—spider mums and gerbera daisies, for example— it's beneficial if each head has been protected with soft mesh or separated from the bunch with a paper collar.

◆ Flowers are graded and priced according to the length of their stems, not by their beauty or popularity. Expect to pay more for any flower with a long stem. With that in mind, you'll appreciate a gift of long-stemmed roses even more.

◆ Don't ever be embarrassed to ask the name of a flower, even if it means pointing to "those little blue bells." Remember that there are hundreds, even thousands, of flowers from around the world, with their myriad names sometimes unknown even by the experts. There's no need to take a crash course in flower identification unless you're planning to open a flower shop. But it is important to build up your flower vocabulary, work with certain flowers a lot, and then move on to expand your flower power.

◆ Speak up if flowers you have bought were below expected standards. Recently, I purchased a dozen champagne roses from my regular greengrocer, whose flowers are usually very healthy. By the next day, most of the heads had drooped. The thought of returning a wilted bouquet

seemed silly, and anyway, how could I prove it wasn't my fault, even though I knew I'd treated my roses with care? When I did report my flowers' untimely demise, the fair-minded merchant apologized and offered me a fresh bunch that looked beautiful all week long.

Cutting (and Recutting)

✦ The stems of most flowers (with certain exceptions that will be discussed later in this book) should be cut or recut at a slant, underwater if possible. Cutting stems underwater prevents air bubbles, which would slow the intake of water, from forming in the stem tissues. Cutting at a slant creates a larger surface area for water intake. In addition to lasting longer, the pointed stem is much easier to push into floral foam.

✦ When the flowers come straight from your garden, be sure to cut them early in the morning or late in the afternoon. Usually there is still moisture on the leaves and flowers, and the sun has not dried the outer cells. Look for the longest, straightest stems, and select blossoms that are just beginning to open.

✦ Proper cutting encourages water intake. Your flowers need to drink as they would in nature. Cutting off their water supply is much like cutting off someone's food and oxygen, so it's important to pay attention to the water for the life of the arrangement.

✦ Cutting straight across the stem is usually best for stems that are tubular or look like straws. These flowers include daffodils, narcissus, and anemones. Because the centers are hollow, air can enter the openings, so place the flowers in water immediately. With this type of stem, water slightly cooler than room temperature is usually preferred.

✦ Large, hollow-stemmed flowers, such as agapanthus, can be held upside down after cutting, then filled with water. If you have the time, plug stems with cotton to keep in the water. The porous cotton will allow the flowers to continuously absorb fresh water from the vase or container.

◆ In the case of bulb flowers, such as tulips and daffodils, cut off the white part of the stem, which cannot absorb water.

◆ A small knife should be used to scrape the stems free of thorns and bumps. The leaves and side shoots that fall below the waterline should be removed from the stem as well to prevent bacteria and bad smells caused by decay. This trimming also allows the flower to drink more water. Save the shoots in a bowl of water for a small bouquet.

◆ The ends of such branches as magnolia, forsythia, mountain laurel, and dogwood should be crushed with a hammer or kitchen mallet and frayed after cutting. Another process that's equally successful entails cutting two or three vertical slits a few inches long at the bottom of the stem with a knife, or crosscutting the diameters. These actions allow for more water absorption by denser, thicker stems.

◆ The ends of flowers with sappy stems, such as poppies and dahlias, should be burned with a match or the flame of a candle to seal the stem and help prevent sap from oozing into the container and clouding the water.

No garden can really be too small to hold a peony.
Had I but four square feet of ground at my disposal,
I would plant a peony in the center and proceed to worship.

Mrs. Edward Harding

◆ Recut stems every day or two to prolong the arrangement's life.

◆ The stamens of lilies—especially the white varieties—provide color, but remember that the pollen stains anything it touches. You may wish to clip off the stamens.

◆ Gently spray any dirt or sand from the stems and leaves of pre-wrapped flowers. Avoid wetting flower heads, which can become water-spotted.

◆ Never use oil or leaf polish on green leaves to clean them or make them shiny. These products close the leaves' pores. Instead, just wipe with mild soap and water if necessary.

Conditioning (and Refreshing)

◆ Plants and flowers are living things, so the temperature of the water for most flowers should be room temperature or warmer, never cold. Cold water will stop flowers' circulation and keep water from traveling up the stems. Just remember it this way: if you cut your finger, an ice cube or cold water helps close pores and stop bleeding. This is good first aid for you, but not for the flowers.

◆ After flowers are cut from the garden or recut they need conditioning in deep water to firm up the stems and revitalize them before any arrangement should be attempted. Conditioning is a simple process but it

takes several hours, so be sure to leave enough time. Place the flowers in a large container filled about three-quarters with water. Many professional florists use only plain water for the conditioning period; however, others suggest adding a flower nutrient to the water—a commercial brand or simply a pinch of sugar (allow approximately one teaspoon per quart or liter)—plus several drops of bleach to hinder the growth of bacteria. Allow the flowers to sit in this conditioning bath for a minimum of four to five hours so that they can draw water and open.

Forsythia is pure joy. There is not an ounce, not a glimmer of sadness or even knowledge in forsythia. Pure, undiluted, untouched joy.

Anonymous

✦ There are several ready-to-use flower foods on the market, such as Floralife, that help eliminate the guesswork.

✦ Never assume that the flowers you buy have already been conditioned unless the person selling them to you can assure you of this.

✦ Condition flowers in a cool, dark place—a garage or a basement is ideal. If you're entertaining on Saturday night, cut or purchase your flowers on Friday morning and condition them until you're ready to start arranging them on Saturday afternoon. By that time the flowers will, in the trade vernacular, have "hardened." Never place flowers in direct sunlight while conditioning or after arranging.

✦ If you need a full-blown bouquet of roses and you're stuck with buds that are just beginning to show color, you can plunge the stems into very warm water and let them sit for four to five hours. This will force the buds to open. This technique also works with certain other flowers, such as mums, daisies, and peonies, and with branches of woody-stemmed flowers, such as forsythia. To stop a flower from opening too quickly, switch to room-temperature water. Sometimes it's prettier to use this forcing technique on only some of the buds. In nature, every flower has its own time schedule, and your bouquet will look more natural this way.

✦ When conditioning flowering branches, such as forsythia and quince, use two tablespoons of bleach for each gallon (3.7L) of water to keep the water fresh and free of bacteria.

✦ If you want to take a walk in the woods to look for flowers, take along a bucket of water and put cut flowers in it immediately. But be warned—many wildflowers are not used for arranging because they simply do not hold up.

✦ If using a metal container for conditioning or arranging, make certain it's galvanized. Tall, cylindrical pails designed for holding and conditioning flowers also come in plastic.

✦ To straighten out crooked stems, wrap an individual stem or the whole bouquet in paper as tightly as possible without damaging the flowers, then secure with string. Place wrapped flowers in a container filled with room-temperature water and leave overnight.

✦ To revive drooping petals, wrap each flower head gently but firmly in paper, making a little collar. Then place the flower stems in warm water up to the necks. In about two hours, the flower heads should revive.

✦ Replenish the water in an arrangement daily. Dumping in a glass of fresh water doesn't really do the job. The flowers drink and water evaporates; water also picks up bacteria. It's necessary to pour out as much of the old water as possible and refill the container with a crystal-clear drink. You should add flower food and

bleach to the water before arranging the flowers and whenever you change the water. Gently coax the flowers back in place, or rearrange them completely.

✦ Once you become more familiar with certain flowers, you can find out about plant foods that are especially suited to them. For example, Canterbury bells like a bit of baking soda in their conditioning water, while bird-of-paradise thrive when a small amount of vinegar is added to the water. But until you know your flowers well enough to cater to their individual needs, a good rule of thumb is to put in a ready-to-use packet of flower food (or sugar as recommended) plus a drop or so of bleach.

✦ When you mist flowers, you deceive them into thinking they're still outside enjoying the morning dew. The mist revives them and helps the buds to open.

✦ Arrangements should last for at least four to five days and possibly up to two weeks, depending, of course, on the flowers and foliage used. Evan G. Hughes says he'll

often take an arrangement of fresh flowers off the dining room table at night and put it in the basement or on the cool enclosed porch until morning "to gain a few more days of life."

TIME-HONORED TECHNIQUES: HELPFUL WAYS TO WORK WITH CUT FLOWERS

Many of my friends belong to garden clubs or have taken courses in flower arranging, so I used to assume that it took time and some special knowledge to make flowers look great. Then, the first time I cut my hydrangeas too short, I placed them in a squatty little bowl and their charming fullness stopped everyone in their tracks. The next week, the elegant long-stemmed hydrangeas that I placed in a tall vase made the room seem absolutely grand. Both arrangements were successes. I've found that there is no "right" way to arrange beautiful flowers and that experience is often the best teacher. With that said, it's also true that knowing a few basics about working with flowers is helpful.

✦ You can arrange the flowers and foliage in your hand first by holding the stems in one hand and gradually adding to them. This is often called a spiraling technique. Begin by holding the first stem at its middle. Angle the second stem diagonally, its head to the left of the first flower head. Continue to add stems diagonally. You can either add the foliage as you go or intersperse it at the end. Use your thumb to hold each stem as it is added. When you're happy with your arrangement, put it into the container. Some people tie a

✦ Most people like to arrange flowers in the container, using a knitting technique in which you continuously add stems by crisscrossing them. Begin by placing the larger foliage in the vase, then add branches and flowers, building a structure as you increase your bouquet. By knitting and balancing your arrangement, you will soon "lock" in your flowers so tightly that even a large arrangement will not topple or wobble. The results will be luxuriant and natural-looking.

string around the bouquet to hold the flowers in place and remove it to loosen the arrangement once the bouquet has been put in a vase.

✦ By using floral foam, frogs and pin holders, chicken wire, or tape, you can give your arrangement more structure. These items work well for some types of minimalist arrangements, such as those inspired by Japanese ikebana, where it's important for every flower and branch to be in a certain position. Be sure to hide the "mechanics" with foliage first. This process is called "greening the container."

✦ I like to use colored marbles, pebbles, seashells, and smooth stones. They help anchor stems and make the arrangement more stable, plus they add a pretty touch to any clear glass container.

✦ Floral wires are used when wiring flowers that need extra stability, especially delicate varieties, and should be secured and covered with corsage tape. Wires can be purchased in various gauges, depending on their use. To secure leaves or moss,

People from a planet without flowers would think we must be mad with joy the whole time to have such things about us.

Iris Murdoch

shape floral wires into hairpin-style hooks, then push them into the foam. These hooks are then pushed down through plant material, such as single leaves or patches of moss.

✦ Floral foam, or Oasis, should be cut into the correct shape for the container, then soaked thoroughly in water before use. After you've secured foam in the container—either by wedging it into place or taping it—add additional water to the container. As the water evaporates, your Oasis will dry out. Be sure to replenish water frequently. If you reuse your floral foam for another arrangement, you risk spreading any plant bacteria that may be lingering from the former arrangement.

chapter two

A Multitude of Flowers

TRICKS OF THE TRADE:
ELEMENTS OF DESIGN

There was a period of time in the recent past when it was all the rage for flower arrangements to look formal and "done," much like hairdos of the same era. Happily, we've moved on to more natural and pleasing styles for both hair and flowers.

Look to the Dutch and Flemish flower painters, the early masters who immortalized floral arrangements in their paintings, for inspiration. (Jan Brueghel and Jan Vermeer are my favorite examples.) Chances are that these artists had not heard about any of the techniques in this book, so relax and begin your lesson here.

I have here only made a nosegay of culled flowers,
and have brought nothing of my own but the thread
that ties them together.

Michel Eyquem de Montaigne

On Shape

✦ Think of how flowers form a kind of triangle as they grow: leaves reach to the sides; the bud or flower is at the top. If you respect the shape nature has given flowers when you place them into a container, you'll have a natural-looking arrangement. You'll see that most arrangements are a variation on this triangle theme.

✦ If the container stands on a hall table or mantel with its back to a wall, arrange from the side that will be seen. If you can see most but not all of the arrangement from where it is placed—on a side table in the living room, for example—be sure to fill in any "holes" with greenery and flowers. If the display is an arrangement that will be viewed from all sides, move the container as you work, and look at it from all angles. This is especially important with basket arrangements.

◆ A one-sided arrangement, or line arrangement, is a Japanese-inspired display of flowers in a staggered vertical row. Stems are generally cut to different lengths. Closed blooms should be kept at the tallest position toward the rear of the display. Keep open blooms shorter and in the front. Arrange spiky leaves in a similar way. If you have used any frogs or pins, you can conceal them with shorter foliage or with decorative stones and marbles.

◆ Decide where your arrangement will go before you select your container and flowers. Does the hall table need tall forsythia to fill in the blank wall space behind it, or would a low cluster of lilacs work better because the wall is very busy? Will a large display overpower the coffee table and make it impossible for people to see each

other? Does that darling teacup filled with spring pansies get lost as a centerpiece?

On Color

◆ Color combinations can be exciting—think of red poppies with orange gerbera daisies. Or they can be calming—imagine a mixture of delphiniums in soft blue and white.

◆ Soft colors often need to be paired with brighter hues to bring out the beauty of both. Think of pale pink roses and larkspur with sassy red snapdragons.

◆ Monochromatic schemes use shades of the same color. A beautiful look can be achieved by including only blue flowers, for example, but in both strong and delicate shades.

◆ Light-hued flowers appear to rush up to greet you, while dark-hued flowers seem to recede.

◆ Sometimes a room's lighting and color scheme will help determine the flower selections. For example, an interior dining area will come to life with white or yellow displays, while a library painted Chinese red may sing "Jingle Bells" in July if the arrangement includes too much green.

On Balance

◆ Visual balance is achieved in a display when vivid flowers are placed in the center and are surrounded by paler colors.

As you add flowers and greenery, avoid a uniform design. Symmetry tends to be boring in flower arranging. Balance is better attained by using plants in a variety of shapes, sizes, colors, and textures.

◆ When arranging flowers and deciding on the placement of groups of containers, work in odd numbers. Three vases on a mantel is a good number. You can avoid an altarlike symmetry that way.

✦ Flowers should never look too "arranged" or overworked. If you feel that a display is stiff-looking, gently play with the stems and loosen them for a more spontaneous look. Remove a few stems and see what happens. It helps if you remind yourself not to try too hard.

✦ A full bouquet doesn't have to be huge to be effective. It's better to arrange flowers so that they can be appreciated individually as well as together, rather than trying for a dramatic display. If it's drama you're after, let longer flowers and branches—forsythia or quince, for example—reach out gracefully. Over-crowded vases are a thing of the past.

✦ Last but not least, talk to your flowers. It may seem like a silly thing to do, but many of the most highly respected floral designers give this advice.

THE FLORAL RAINBOW: A COLOR CHART

When buying flowers for a special occasion, some people like to make a shopping list in advance and think about the many wonderful combinations. This flower color chart includes the most popular and widely used flowers grouped by color. The list is by no means the final word; however, you should find most of your old friends here, plus a few new ones.

White Hues

amaryllis	gladiolus
anemone	grape hyacinth
apple blossom	heather
aster	lily-of-the-valley
astilbe	magnolia
baby's breath	narcissus (paper-white)
bellflower	
calla lily	nigella (love-in-a-mist)
camellia	orchid
candytuft	pansy
Canterbury bell	phlox
carnation	primrose
chrysanthemum	Queen Anne's lace
clematis	ranunculus
columbine	rhododendron
cornflower (bachelor's button)	rose
	snapdragon
cosmos	spirea
dahlia	statice
daisy	stock
delphinium	sweet pea
dogwood	sweet William
feverfew	tuberose
freesia	tulip
gardenia	viburnum (snowball)
gentian	wisteria
gerbera daisy	zinnia

Yellow and Orange Hues

buttercup	lupine
calendula	marigold
chrysanthemum	nasturtium
cockscomb	pansy
columbine	phlox
dahlia	poppy
delphinium	primrose
forsythia	ranunculus
freesia	rose
gerbera daisy	snapdragon
gladiolus	stock
goldenrod	sunflower
hyacinth	tulip
iris	yarrow
lily	zinnia

Orange and Orange-Red Hues

bird-of-paradise	nasturtium
Chinese lantern	peony
chrysanthemum	poppy
cosmos	pyracantha
dahlia	(firethorn)
fritillaria	ranunculus
gerbera daisy	salvia
gladiolus	snapdragon
lily	zinnia

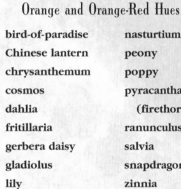

Red Hues

amaryllis	lily
anemone	lobelia
azalea	peony
carnation	primrose
cockscomb	rose
dahlia	snapdragon
freesia	stock
gerbera daisy	sweet pea
gladiolus	sweet William
hollyhock	zinnia

Dark Orange and Brown Hues

chrysanthemum	iris
cockscomb	lily
coreopsis	marigold
freesia	pansy
gerbera daisy	rose
hydrangea	zinnia

Pink Hues

aster	larkspur
Canterbury bell	lily
carnation	lupine
chrysanthemum	orchid
columbine	peony
cornflower	phlox
cosmos	poppy
cottage pink	ranunculus
dahlia	rose
foxglove	scabiosa
freesia	snapdragon
gerbera daisy	stock
gladiolus	sweet pea
heather	sweet William
hollyhock	tulip
hyacinth	verbena
hydrangea	zinnia

Blue Hues

ageratum	grape hyacinth
allium	hyacinth
anemone	hydrangea
aster	iris
bellflower	larkspur
bergamot	nigella
Canterbury bell	pansy
clematis	phlox
columbine	primrose
cornflower	scabiosa
cosmos	stock
delphinium	sweet pea
forget-me-not	thistle
gentian	Tibetan poppy
gladiolus	veronica (speedwell)

Roses, like debutantes, do not appear
unannounced.
They must be formally presented to the
public.

Thomas Christopher

Purple Hues

anemone

aster

bellflower

Canterbury bell

columbine

cosmos

dahlia

delphinium

foxglove

freesia

gentian

gladiolus

heather

iris

larkspur

lavender

lilac

lupine

orchid

pansy

rose

scabiosa (pincushion)

sweet pea

violet

wisteria

As inscribed in Mary Ella Bechtel's
    autograph book:
Life's field will yield as we make it
    A harvest of thorns or of flowers.
Your friend,

                    Howard R. Teavy
                    June 10, 1887

Green Hues

bearded iris

bells-of-Ireland

button chrysanthemum

cymbidium orchid

early hydrangea

gladiolus

lady's-mantle

Lenten rose

parrot tulip

rose

zinnia

WOODLAND ACCESSORIES: FOLIAGE, TWIGS, AND BRANCHES

Not too many years ago, flower arrangements consisted of predictable flowers and a few greens, mostly ferns. Today when we think about arranging flowers, we consider a range of foliage in addition to the exciting variety of twigs and branches that help us create truly natural arrangements.

Greens and Natural Foliage

artichoke leaves	hydrangea leaves
bear grass	ivy
berries that are unripe	jasmine tendrils
boxwood	laurel
carrot tops	lemon leaves
cattail	mosses
dill	myrtle palms
eucalyptus	pine
evergreens	privet
fennel	salal tips
ferns	shrimp plant
fishtail palms	silver dollar
holly	timothy
huckleberry leaves	vinca vine (periwinkle)

Twigs and Branches

apple blossom	flowering almond
barberry	forsythia
beech twigs	jack-o'-lantern
birch twigs	Japanese maple
blackberries on their stems	larch twigs
cherry blossom	pussy willow
corylopsis (winter hazel)	quince
curly hazel twigs	redbud
curly willow	rose branches with rosehips
daphne	Scotch broom
dogwood	smoke bush
	witch hazel

chapter three

Ideas for Holders and Arrangements

CONTAINER SENSE:
ADVICE ABOUT TRADITIONAL CHOICES

The bouquet is the star, but the container has a very important supporting role. In a successful arrangement, the size, shape, and color of the vessel complement the flowers but the vessel never steals the limelight from them. The right container can make all the difference between a pleasing arrangement and one that looks unbalanced and disappointing. This section provides a variety of helpful tips on containers—from tried-and-true crystal vases to old cowboy boots—and advice about how to work with them.

✦ To a great extent, the proportions of the container dictate the types of flowers suited to it, and vice versa. Just one good look at a vase's mouth, height, shape, and overall size should give you a good idea of whether those wonderful long pussy willow branches will look graceful or just plain leggy.

✦ Arrangements will lean and bend over the edges of a flared vase. Avoid stiff-stemmed flowers that don't respond to a graceful curve, though these may work nicely in the center. Put foliage and low flowers in first.

✦ A compact display of short flowers in a low, wide cylindrical vase is easy and irresistible. Place this type of display where it will be viewed from above. Tall, narrow cylindrical vases allow flowers and foliage to extend far beyond the sides, but arrangements can be more impressive if kept somewhat restrained. Long, elegant stems, such as lilies, are wonderful in this type of vase. Foliage inserted at the base of the arrangement can balance the display and cascade down over the rim gracefully.

✦ Hourglass-shaped vases come in an exciting variety, but you should make certain that the stems will be held by the narrow place in the center and not by the flared rim of the vase.

✦ Flowers arranged in small, low bowls should be kept compact, with larger flowers placed more centrally. Smaller heads, buds, and willowy foliage can lean over the edge of the bowl. Larger bowls function in much the same way, except that very wide openings may require a grid of tape for this fuller arrangement.

times the height of the container. Use this rule as a starting point, then find the height that's right for your special arrangement.

✦ Bud vases hold a little and say a lot. Diverge from the traditional rosebud and pack these miniature containers with many tiny flowers, such as lily-of-the-valley or baby's breath.

✦ Sometimes an exceptional container threatens to steal the show. To create a balance, pair it with breathtaking white orchids or an amaryllis with several blooms in progress.

✦ Sometimes, trial and error is the only way to be sure about successful matches of flowers and containers. A sleek, black modernist vase would probably look more suitable with dramatic trumpet lilies than with cheerful zinnias; however, it's always best to try out such combinations.

✦ The container's height and overall stability should tell you how large your flowers can be before the arrangement takes a tumble or simply looks overdone. The traditional rule of thumb is that flowers should be no more than one and a half

◆ A glass container, whether it's a splendid Victorian cut-glass vase or a smart contemporary cube, rarely competes with your flowers and foliage. It also reveals the interesting underside of the arrangement and allows you to show off stones, marbles, and other decorative touches beneath the water's surface. Clear glass is not a good choice if you need to hide the mechanics of the display, such as the floral foam or wire.

◆ Frosted glass containers can offer interesting texture, as well as a visually heavier base than a clear glass container. Another plus is that the mechanics of the arrangement are hidden.

◆ Patterned antique china containers can be a bit busy, but everyone seems to love the fresh blue and white designs. With these vessels, a monochromatic color scheme in flowers can be extremely effective.

◆ No one needs convincing that baskets, with their many colors, textures, shapes, and sizes, are some of the most charming

and inviting of the popular containers. What would florists do without them? Sometimes baskets designed for flower arrangements come with heavy plastic liners. If yours is lacking a preformed liner, it's important to find a good strong

piece of plastic, or a plastic or glass bowl that fits snugly to prevent leakage. A block of floral foam should be taped to the liner to hold it securely.

✦ It's smart to keep your most-used containers together in one place. Dedicate a pantry or closet shelf to these favorite standbys. It's helpful when you don't have to turn the whole house upside down to find the perfect container.

✦ Don't put your most cherished containers behind closed doors. A colorful majolica vase or a stylized Arts and Crafts vessel makes a stunning objet d'art, with or without flowers.

✦ Make certain you love the vase as much as the flowers. And have fun! The rules are there to be pushed and broken. No one's handing out grades.

CONTAINER CREATIONS: UNIQUE HOLDERS TO FIND AND MAKE

Expand your definition of "container" by adding unusual and whimsical possibilities to the list of traditional vases and vessels. Look around your home for wonderful objects, and press them into a new use. Consider fruits and vegetables that might be turned into vessels. Or create your own imaginative holders that quickly establish a certain mood or style.

This profusion of ideas comes from my home, as well as from friends and relatives who are always very nice about sharing. I'd like to brag that I've wowed my guests with the many ideas that follow, yet I haven't begun to make a dent in the wonderful possibilities.

Around the House and Garden

◆ Brightly colored coffee mugs can be used alone or clustered on a tabletop. Use antique teacups for a more sophisticated look. Demitasse cups are perfect for diminutive rosebuds, lily-of-the-valley sprays, or pansies.

◆ The lovely china soup tureen that is sitting pretty on the sideboard would look even prettier if it held a mix of pink, purple, and white cosmos from the garden or the season's first lilacs in bloom.

◆ Abandoned rubber boots (one or the pair) need only sunflowers or hollyhocks to turn them into vessels that quickly become a conversation piece. If necessary, place stones in the toe of a boot for added stability, then set a tall container of water inside the boot. Old cowboy boots, work boots, and even baby shoes are also fun, unexpected containers.

◆ Baking tins and pans are available in many novelty shapes in addition to the standard round and square ones. Remember to safeguard surfaces first by lining them with plastic. Add floral foam if necessary, then tape in place. Fill tins with masses of low flowers to conform to the shape. Your daughter's ballet recital is the perfect occasion for a star design; try a heart for Valentine's Day. Never arrange your flowers in an ungalvanized metal container without using a liner. A wide ribbon or strip of fabric can hide any part of the container that may show.

✦ Cheerfully decorated food tins—once you've finished the olive oil, amaretto cookies, or loose tea—are great for showing off such flowers as sassy daisies and exuberant red poppies. Since food tins are usually bright and busy, you may want to stick to a simple design scheme: one variety of flower or one color. These arrangements are most successful when the flowers are massed tightly and pro-

trude several inches above the container's rim. A small bundle of raffia can be twisted, then wrapped and knotted loosely around the stems just above the edge of the tin.

✦ Candleholders minus the candles make charming diminutive containers and are perfect for festive occasions. Make sure that smaller holders have enough room for a small piece of floral foam, shaped to fit, and be sure that water won't damage the holders. If you use a clear glass holder, tie a ribbon to camouflage the interior, or arrange greens and vines so that they trail over the sides.

✦ There are clever, circular plastic candle vases that slip over a candle and rest on the top of the candleholder. These devices hold water and provide holes all the way around for small flowers.

✦ A creel is a wicker basket intended to hold fish, but the addition of a plastic liner and a block of floral foam transforms it into an unusual rustic vessel for an arrangement. Sit it on a table or hang it on a wall.

◆ Converting an old tennis racket into a flower container may sound slightly implausible, yet it makes the perfect holder for that victory party after the big match. Wire a water-soaked floral foam block wrapped in plastic to a tennis racket. Poke flowers and foliage of your choice into the foam (those sharply cut stems are doubly helpful in this situation). Fresh flowers in this tennis bouquet tend to fade when the foam dries out, making this type of arrangement a fun game, but possibly a short match.

◆ A bird's nest can be a wonderful addition to an arrangement, but please don't take one from a tree. It's much friendlier to the environment to use one from a crafts supply store—many stores stock them. A small lightweight nest can be settled among the branches of a woodland arrangement for an unusual naturalistic touch. Some people like to spray-paint nests silver or gold to make them sparkle for the holidays.

◆ Medicine bottles in clear or muted tones of blue, green, and amber can be picked up at flea markets and antique

shops. Faithful reproductions are easily found in garden shops and catalogs. Let each dinner guest enjoy an exclusive flower arrangement. At the end of the meal, announce that every arrangement is a gift. Another idea is to cluster medicine bottles in the center of the table. Because you can always find a place for little bottles in tight quarters, I like to set them on bathroom vanities and night tables for color and warmth, or line them up on a windowsill. The light plays magically off the old glass.

The violet is for faithfulness,
    Which in me shall abide;
Hoping, likewise, from your heart
    You will not let it slide.

J.S. Ogilvie

✦ Glass Victorian bulb containers in pretty colors double as charming vases for cut flowers.

✦ Large jugs and crocks make perfect floor vases. Set them on a stair landing or in an entrance hall. Fill them with tall pussy willow, cattail, hydrangea, or ornamental grasses. Long-lasting flowers and greenery are good choices for these large vases, especially those that look good as they dry naturally in the container.

✦ Roses and silver are a winning combination. Dust off that silver high school trophy cup that you've so modestly put away in a closet and fill it with a bouquet of roses.

✦ A delightful folk art piece, such as a toy wagon, can become your centerpiece container. Just be sure to line the piece accordingly to protect it and the table.

✦ After my last goldfish (and any further interest in raising fish) had expired, I wondered what to do with the big bowl. Then I picked dozens of bold zinnias and recycled the fishbowl, pebbles and all.

✦ Press into service a brandy glass for a small but elegant arrangement. Just one look through your china cabinet—or a walk through a large store's crystal department—will open your eyes to all sorts of terrific pieces that work wonderfully as vases. Everything from simple jelly glasses to dramatic champagne flutes can be called into service.

✦ Rustic boxes found at garage sales and flea markets are perfect containers for arrangements of holly or greenery during the winter months.

✦ It's time to buff up the silver wedding gifts and put them to new uses as containers for flowers. Remember those julep cups from your aunt?

✦ Posy holders are the delicate cone-shaped flower containers that were popular during the Victorian era, when women carried flowers as they would carry a handbag or pinned these little vases to their clothing like brooches. Also called tussie-mussies, these collectible objects—most often made of silver or gold and embellished with gems and mother-of-pearl—are making a comeback in flower arranging. Posy holders that have their own tripod-like stands can be set on a table upright and filled with fresh flowers. Those with handles, or the pin-on variety, may also be filled with dried flowers and placed on a formal dinner table by each place setting, like floral cornucopias.

✦ The ubiquitous terra-cotta flowerpot can double as a container for fresh cut flowers.

Slip a glass or plastic liner inside the pot, arrange with flowers, and close any remaining gaps between the pot and the stems with moss.

✦ Many types of leaves can be hot-glued onto the outside of a glass, jar, or inexpensive vase. Look for autumn leaves that are not too brittle. Try galax leaves, which dry well, or banana leaves, which wrap easily.

In gardening, I try to paint living pictures with flowers, paying
attention to throwing them into groups both for form and color.

Gertrude Jekyll

◆ Small galvanized tin pails filled with sunflowers make captivating centerpieces for a country wedding reception.

◆ For more formal arrangements, bring a classical garden urn indoors and create an exuberant large-scale arrangement using a bold collection of flowers—such as delphinium, lilies, roses, anemones, lilacs, tulips, peonies, and dogwood—mixed with lush greens, grasses, and twisted willow. Fill in any gaps with dill, fennel, and smaller flowers such as lily-of-the-valley and forget-me-nots.

◆ One of my own personal favorites for arranging flowers quickly and simply is my eight-bottle wine basket with fixed double handles. I fill some or all of the bottle openings with tall plain drinking glasses, then fill these with flowers. In March, my wine basket becomes a field of sunny daffodils; in July, it holds a bed of brilliant blue irises; and in August, it boasts a merry mix from the entire garden. This is one of the easiest containers to use, and it gives such joyful results!

◆ One of the most practical and winning vessels is the utilitarian galvanized steel flower pail that's designed to hold and transport just-cut flowers. Tall flowers look elegant in these pails, as do loose and unstructured arrangements. These containers are available through many of the better gardening catalogs.

◆ If you run across an antique inkwell at a good price, snap it up. It makes a novel container for tiny flowers.

✦ An impulsive shopper I know found a dozen amber shot glasses in a junk store and immediately bought them all. When she needed a quick floral touch for a luncheon table, she popped a daisy or two, snipped very short, into each little glass. Then she scattered them up and down the table. Her whimsical arrangement was a hit, her capricious purchase justified.

Holders from Fruits and Vegetables

✦ A pumpkin makes a bold and appealing receptacle for fall occasions. Simply cut off the top and hollow the pumpkin out as you would for a jack-o'-lantern. This setup can probably hold water for a number of days, but it's best to use a liner to keep the pumpkin from rotting. With very large pumpkins, floral foam may be helpful. Everyone loves flowers in harvest colors, such as chrysanthemums, mop-head hydrangeas, sunflowers, and fiery orange red-hot pokers.

✦ Look around the produce department and the vegetable garden for more container ideas. Melons and squash make

unusual vessels year-round, as do bell peppers, cabbage, and eggplant. In fact, an eggplant adds great color and looks stunning with lilacs. Handle it as you would a pumpkin. Floral foam is helpful in smaller vegetable containers.

✦ As the grand finale of his lecture on creative flower arranging, floral designer Evan G. Hughes comes through with the pièce de résistance for a Thanksgiving table's centerpiece: hollow out a large loaf of bread, round or oblong. Then fill the space with a plastic liner containing floral foam. Arrange autumn flowers coupled with stems of dried wheat. The leftover bread can be shredded and used for the stuffing. You end up with no waste and a certain conversation piece!

Making the Unusual Holder

✦ If you can wrap a gift, you can wrap a length a of pretty floral fabric around a plain container and tie it with strips cut from the fabric with pinking shears, a bit of decorative fringe, or a contrasting ribbon. For your arrangement, select flowers that pick up one or two of the livelier colors in the print. Just remember that the busier the fabric pattern, the simpler your choice of flowers should be.

✦ Silver or gold lamé fabric changes a plain-Jane glass into a Cinderella vase. Secure the fabric to the glass by circling it with bands of thin gold thread or cord, or hot-glue the fabric to the container. By winding beautiful wide ribbon around a plain glass, you can also create an elegant and inexpensive vase.

✦ With twigs of approximately the same length and a smooth-sided glass, you can make your own rustic twig container. Simply hot-glue the twigs to the glass, one after the other, until you've completed the circle. Add a decorative raffia tie or a simple bow. You can also create this country-style vase using thin bamboo, narrow strips of bark, cinnamon sticks, or even chopsticks.

✦ Many flowers dry well right in the container without any special preparation. The best candidates are flowers whose heads won't droop, such as hydrangea, statice, and baby's breath. For wonderful ideas on using dried flowers in wreaths, read *The Ultimate Wreath Book* by Ellen Specter.

♦ Any ordinary brown paper grocery bag can be turned into a display package for flowers. Just slip a pot or bowl into the bag, and, crumpling the paper as you work, roll down the bag to the rim of the pot. Tie raffia or a ribbon around the bag, and you're all set. The paper bag theme is a good one for a child's party. Any child will love being involved in coloring the paper bag and helping you create the container. Try crumpling a small brown lunch bag around a chunky glass or a mason jar. Group several on a table. Fresh country flowers such as marigolds, daisies, and zinnias suit this easygoing arrangement best. If it's even more color you're after, look for the brightly lacquered bags at party and crafts stores. Affix a bunch of balloons with yards of curly ribbon and you're ready for a party.

♦ A wonderful bridal or baby shower arrangement is a nosegay bouquet, which afterward becomes the perfect gift for the guest of honor. Arrange your bouquet with lovely yet sturdy flowers, such as violets, tulips, and freesia, or flowers that dry well, such as hydrangea and lavender. Wrap the stems in water-soaked cotton wadding, and place in a plastic bag. Secure with a rubber band or string. You're now ready to wrap your bouquet in colored tissue, shiny foil, or crisp fabric. Tie with raffia or ribbon. A nosegay is pretty on a table or atop the biggest gift box. Naturally, it won't last as long as a bouquet in a container of water, but it can always be unwrapped and placed in a vase after the party.

♦ Cut all the stems of a daffodil bouquet the same length, leaving them as long as possible. Wrap a band around the bouquet about two-thirds of the way down the stems, using raffia, ribbon, long grasses, or a flexible leaf, such as galax or dracaena.

Fill a decorative soup bowl—a softly colored Chinese bowl is just the right size and shape—with water and place a heavy pin or frog in it. Jam the cut stems into the pin as far as they will go to secure the topiary-style arrangement. Cover the frog and the bowl bottom with polished stones or white gravel. Watch the water level carefully, and refresh the bowl often.

♦ Create a unique version of a festooned hurricane lamp using a large glass hurricane shade, a small galvanized tin pail, and a tall candle. Place the shade in the center of the pail with the candle inside. Build a pyramid of kumquats around the candle; this will hold the candle straight as well as decorate the interior. Then create a wreath by tucking snippets of greenery, such as boxwood or laurel leaves, around the candle—between the pail and the glass. Surround the pail with a still life of oranges, limes, pears, and, of course, kumquats.

♦ Pieces of large, hollow bamboo can be the basis for an exotic container. Plug up one end with florist clay to prevent leaks; put a small piece of floral foam in the other (top) end; then add a few flowers and twigs. Group three or more of these "vases" together, each cut at a different level, and bind with raffia or a strong vine such as grapevine. If you're worried about a table surface, place a pretty saucer or plate under the arrangement.

SHOWING OFF NATURALLY: INCORPORATING ELEMENTS FROM NATURE

Clear glass and Lucite containers are wonderful when you want to show off natural "props" that enhance arrangements. In many instances, these natural elements help hold a display together by adding color, texture, and interest.

✦ To create a scented display, set a glass container within a larger glass container. The space in between the two—from one to three inches (2.5 to 7.5cm) is ideal—becomes a kind of empty "moat" to be filled with fragrant potpourri. The soft colors of the dried petals team up with the scent to make a heady combination. When the fragrance fades, the potpourri can be refreshed with scented oils. The potpourri stays dry as your fresh flower arrangement thrives in the inner vase.

✦ Clear and colored marbles are both attractive and useful: they stabilize the stems and decorate the glass vase. Stones, small shells, and pebbles act in much the same way. They can also lie outside the container on the table as part of an earthy still-life arrangement.

And the fruits will outdo what the flowers have promised.

François de Malherbe

✦ Fresh cranberries placed in the bottom of a glass vase add festive color and help to anchor the arrangement.

✦ Fresh orange, lemon, and lime slices can be slipped between a cushion of moss and the sides of a plain glass vase. Ball-shaped vases with wide necks are especially effective for this type of arrangement. Don't forget to remove the seeds.

✦ Dried fruit can be placed in the part of your arrangement that's above water. Citrus slices have lovely colors and textures. Settle them among flowers and greens, or wire them into the arrangement.

✦ Pecans and walnuts have attractive hulls, as do many other nuts. Consider wiring them onto an arrangement or scattering them on the table as part of a still-life effect.

✦ Tie a bundle of cinnamon sticks onto a container with fancy ribbon.

✦ Add natural accents in the form of dried pomegranates and poppy seed heads. Many other fruits and vegetables are delightfully ornamental and also hold up well. These include artichokes, both small and large, with their rugged good looks; small gourds, whose curvy shapes and deep waxy colors add to any harvest table; and bunches of small green bananas for tropical arrangements. Kumquats, clementines, lady apples, and star fruit provide colorful and unusual adornment as well. Place in or near the arrangement, or when necessary, wire and add.

◆ You need to experiment with selections from the produce department to discover which fruits and vegetables can last without water in a basket arrangement, which need a cool drink, and which can be submerged without clouding the water or wilting. So much depends on the weather, the condition of the "prop" when you buy it, and its ability to successfully make the transition from dinner plate to centerpiece.

◆ Beet greens, baby lettuces, brussels sprouts on the stem, or small peppers on the stem add an unusual dimension to floral arrangements and have the same water requirements as flowers.

BLUE-RIBBON IDEAS: ARRANGEMENT TIPS AND FLOWER COMBINATIONS

My artist friend Charles Muise says he clips some of his best ideas from magazines. His advice is to dog-ear any page that looks inviting (if you keep your magazines) or rip out anything that seems promising and use it to start a file on flowers. Check out flower shop windows, attend flower shows, and get ideas at friends' parties and weddings.

◆ Sometimes a gift arrangement will arrive from a floral designer's shop complete with tiny leakproof vials (called water pix) encasing individual stems in the arrangement. I always hoard these vials. They come in handy for arranging single flowers in containers that do not tolerate water. Try tucking single blooms of purple and white orchids under the rim of a serving plate that rests on a buffet table, hiding each stem and vial from view. Make a bundt cake for dessert and pop a few non-poisonous flowers (such as nasturtiums or Johnny-jump-ups) in the center. Or insert

Small service is true service while it lasts:

Of humblest friends, bright creature! scorn not one:

The daisy, by shadow that it casts,

Protects the lingering dewdrop from the sun.

William Wordsworth

the pix into flowerpots containing live green plants—your ivy can suddenly bloom with pansies. These vials are also available in several sizes from florist wholesalers.

✦ Place a large-scale arrangement on a pedestal in a corner or in the entrance hall. It doesn't have to be a formal arrangement: a high basket filled with daisies can be striking.

✦ During a long and freezing January, I was disappointed by the lack of fresh blooms available, so I decided to try a mostly-greens arrangement. I purchased the foliage from a flower shop that sells individual stems, and like a kid in a candy shop, I got some of this and some of that: lemon leaves, boxwood, dill heads, laurel, fern, eucalyptus, a shot of silver dollar, and pussy willow. My winter arrangement was more economical than the same quantity of flowers would have been, and it lasted well over two weeks. In the fall, colorful leaves can heighten this kind of long-lasting arrangement.

✦ Branches from a snowball bush in a sleek black Art Deco vase create a sophisticated and romantic arrangement.

✦ Bittersweet is stunning in a blue delft vase.

✦ An all-white mantel arrangement is perfect for many occasions—try roses, freesia, snapdragons, and tulips mixed with greens. Tape a block of wet floral foam, covered with plastic, to a tray or sheet of heavy plastic that has been put in place on the mantel. Arrange the tall flowers toward the back for height and stability. Lightweight foliage and flowers can cascade over the front of the mantel-piece. This concept can also be used to create a stunning display down the center of a buffet table.

✦ A ring of colorful mums is tried-and-true, especially around the base of a candle. Use a ring of floral foam that has been fully saturated with water. Place on a saucer and secure with florist tape. A good plant to start with is moss, attached with floral wire. The flowers and the foliage follow.

✦ Eucalyptus leaves are perfect by themselves in a tall, rounded vase; their swordlike leaves provide an interesting contrast to the container.

✦ Look for special places to put diminutive arrangements of little flowers like daisies

or feverfew: a cluttered workstation; the top of a toilet tank; a windowsill; the shelf of a bookcase; the dashboard of a car (in a special flower container designed for this purpose); a cupboard with glass doors; a tray of hors d'oeuvres; and so on.

✦ Float such flowers as camellias, gardenias, and magnolias in low bowls. Add tiny votive candles designed to float on water for a theatrical centerpiece.

✦ Add a bit of whimsy to an arrangement by including a single different flower, perhaps a miniature sunflower or a bright red poppy.

✦ Ranunculus are reminiscent of the painter Redon. Their twisty stems are part of their great charm. Mix the colors, keep it simple, and don't try to tame them.

✦ Baby's breath may be all that's needed in the big basket in the hallway.

✦ For Valentine's Day, try a passionate mix of miniature carnations: red, hot pink, orange...the works! Or cut a heart out of floral foam and cover it with a variety of miniature carnations to make a floral valentine.

✦ Everyone loves roses when they're in full bloom. Cut the stems short so that they just peek over the top of a stout vase. Display on a stack of books. This is a time when you want your arrangement to look a bit crowded.

✦ Sometimes one stem to a vase is perfection—think of just one calla lily in a tall silver trumpet vase.

✦ When your toddler has outgrown the silver drinking cup, use it for small red roses.

✦ Try purple foxglove in a white pitcher. Cut stems one and a half times as high as the container.

✦ Flowering herbs can add spontaneity to an arrangement—try lavender, calamint, or marjoram.

✦ Remember the kitchen herbs: rosemary, thyme, sage, parsley, and dill. Put them in drinking glasses and set them on the kitchen counter to use for cooking and to show them off.

✦ Tie bouquets of flowers to the backs of chairs for a party, particularly one that is held in the garden.

✦ Forsythia or quince in a large garden urn can look both sweet and grand.

✦ Make sure that your centerpieces are short enough for guests to see each other. A low arrangement is often best—in a basket or in a line of small vessels.

✦ Hydrangea, pale roses, and lilies make a very romantic arrangement.

✦ While you have to be careful not to go bow-crazy, ribbons and flowers are a magical combination. Ribbons can be plaid and innocent or gold and sophisticated. French ribbon is exquisite with its useful wired edges. Keep a bow basket with your flower arranging tools. Add to

it as you find ribbons that appeal to you. Raffia is always great to have on hand—it comes in a wide variety of colors and can be both formal and casual.

✦ For a real holiday splurge, buy freshly cut stems of deep red amaryllis. Make sure that the stems are as long as possible and the vase is sturdy enough to support them. Fortunately, amaryllis are long-lasting, so you'll get to use them for more than one holiday occasion.

✦ An arrangement composed solely of twigs is perfect in the winter. Add winterberries and juniper berries for color.

chapter four

Floral Symbolism

HAPPY BIRTHDAY! A CALENDAR OF FLOWERS

Birthstones are one way of noting your birthday, but birth flowers are an even better way. Here are the birth flowers for every month of the year.

JANUARY—Carnation

FEBRUARY—Violet

MARCH—Jonquil

APRIL—Sweet pea

MAY—Lily-of-the-valley

JUNE—Rose

JULY—Larkspur

AUGUST—Gladiolus

SEPTEMBER—Aster

OCTOBER—Calendula (or marigold)

NOVEMBER—Chrysanthemum

DECEMBER—Narcissus

THE MEANING OF FLOWERS: A SPECIAL LANGUAGE

You have probably heard the old saying that a red rose speaks of love, but roses are not the only flowers that "talk" for us. Select flowers from this list and arrange them together so that your next bouquet can really say something special.

ALMOND BLOSSOM — Sweetness; hope

AMARANTHUS — Immortality

AMARYLLIS — Pride; pastoral poetry

ANEMONE — Withered hopes; forsaken

ANGELICA — Inspiration

APPLE BLOSSOM — Preference

ASTER — Symbol of love; daintiness

AZALEA — Take care of yourself for me; Chinese symbol of womanhood

BEGONIA — Beware

BELLFLOWER — Gratitude

BITTERSWEET — Truth

BLUEBELL — Constancy

BOUQUET OF WITHERED FLOWERS — Rejected love

BROOM — Humility

BUTTERCUP — Childhood

CAMELLIA — Perfection; good-luck gift for a man

CANDYTUFT — Indifference

CARNATION (general) — Fascination

CARNATION (pink) — I'll never forget you

CARNATION (red) — Admiration

CARNATION (striped) — Refusal

CARNATION (white) — Innocence; pure love

CARNATION (yellow) — You have disappointed me; rejection

CATTAIL — Peace; prosperity

CHRYSANTHEMUM (red) — I love you

CHRYSANTHEMUM (white) — Truth

CHRYSANTHEMUM (yellow) — Slighted love

COLUMBINE — Folly

CORNFLOWER — Delicacy

COTTAGE PINK — Divine love

CROCUS — Gladness

CYCLAMEN — Resignation

DAFFODIL — Unrequited love

DAISY — Innocence

DANDELION — Faithfulness; happiness

FERN — Magic; grace

FLAX — Domestic symbol

FORGET-ME-NOT — True love; remembrance

FORSYTHIA — Anticipation

FOXGLOVE — Insincerity

FREESIA — Trust

GARDENIA — Femininity

GERANIUM — Stupidity; folly

GLADIOLUS — Incarnation

GLOXINIA — Love at first sight

HAWTHORN BLOSSOM — Hope

HEATHER (lavender) — Solitude

HEATHER (white) — Protection

HOLLY — Divinity; defense; domestic happiness

HOLLYHOCK — Female ambition

HONEYSUCKLE — Devotion

HUCKLEBERRY — Faith

HYACINTH (blue) — Consistency

HYACINTH (pink or red) — Playfulness

HYACINTH (white) — Loveliness

HYACINTH (yellow) — Jealousy

HYDRANGEA — Heartlessness

IRIS — Your friendship means so much

IVY — Eternal fidelity

JONQUIL — Desire for a return of affection

LARKSPUR — Fickleness

LAVENDER — Devotion; virtue

LILAC (purple) — First emotions

LILAC (white) — Youthful innocence

LILY (calla) — Beauty

LILY (day) — Chinese symbol for mother

LILY (eucharis) — Maiden charms

LILY (tiger) — Wealth; pride; prosperity

LILY (orange) — Hatred

LILY (white) — Purity

LILY (yellow) — Falsehood; gaiety

LILY-OF-THE-VALLEY — Return of happiness

MAGNOLIA — Grief; pride; nobility

MARIGOLD — Joy

MICHAELMAS DAISY — Farewell

MISTLETOE — Love; kiss me

MOCK ORANGE — Deceit

MOSS — Maternal love

MYRTLE — Love; Hebrew symbol of marriage

NARCISSUS — Formality; conceit

NASTURTIUM — Patriotism; victory in battle

OLEANDER — Caution

ORANGE BLOSSOM — Purity; loveliness

ORCHID — Refinement; beauty; Chinese symbol for many children

PALM LEAF — Victory; success

PANSY — Love; merriment; thinking of you

PEACH BLOSSOM — Long life

PEONY — Bashfulness

PERIWINKLE (blue) — Early friendship

PERIWINKLE (white) — Pleasures of memory

PETUNIA — Resentment; anger

POINSETTIA — Fertility; eternity

POPPY (red) — Pleasure

POPPY (white) — Consolation

POPPY (yellow) — Wealth

PRIMROSE — I can't live without you

ROSE (single full bloom) — I love you

ROSE (thornless) — Love at first sight

ROSE (damask) — Persian ambassador of love

ROSE (dark crimson) — Mourning

ROSE (pink) — Perfect happiness; please believe me

ROSE (red) — Love; passion

ROSE (white) — Innocence; purity

ROSE (yellow) — Jealousy

ROSEBUD — Beauty; youth

SALVIA (red) — I am thinking of you

SNAPDRAGON — Deception; strength

STEPHANOTIS — Happiness in marriage

STOCK — Bond of affection

SUNFLOWER — Haughtiness; false riches

SWEET PEA — Departure

TULIP (general) — Flower emblem of Holland; fame

TULIP (red) — Declaration of love

TULIP (variegated) — Beautiful eyes

TULIP (yellow) — Hopeless love

VIOLET (general) — Humility

VIOLET (blue) — Faithfulness

VIOLET (white) — Let's take a chance on happiness

VISCARIA — Will you dance with me?

WALLFLOWER — Fidelity in adversity

WINTERGREEN — Harmony

WISTERIA — Welcome

ZINNIA (general) — Thinking of absent friends

ZINNIA (magenta) — Lasting affection

ZINNIA (scarlet) — Constancy

ZINNIA (white) — Goodness

ZINNIA (yellow) — Daily remembrance

The red rose whispers of passion
    And the white rose breathes of love

O, the red rose is a falcon,
    And the white rose is a dove.

John Boyle O'Reilly

THE FLOWER ARRANGING RECORD BOOK: A DIARY AND KEEPER

Just as I try to avoid serving the same dish to my dinner guests twice in a row, so do I vary the centerpiece. Having a special place to jot down a few thoughtful notes is all it takes. A flower diary helps keep track of arrangements and much more. This is the information I keep in mine:

ARRANGEMENTS

Date

Occasion

Description

Flowers and Container Comments

Sketch/Photo

FLOWERS

Name/Description

Where to Buy

When in Season

Comments

FLOWER ROLODEX

Flower Shop/Market/Garden Center

Address

Phone

Fax